The Successful Team-Building Workbook

Self-Assessments, Exercises & Educational Handouts

Ester A. Leutenberg
John J. Liptak, EdD

Illustrated by
Amy L. Brodsky, LISW

Whole Person Associates
Duluth, Minnesota

Whole Person Associates
101 W. 2nd St., Suite 203
Duluth, MN 55802

800-247-6789

books@wholeperson.com
www.wholeperson.com

The Successful Team-Building Workbook
Self-Assessments, Exercises & Educational Handouts

Printed in the United States of America

10 9 8 7 6 5 4 3 2 1

Editorial Director: Carlene Sippola
Art Director: Joy Morgan Dey

Library of Congress Control Number: 2008942512
ISBN: 978-1-57025-230-3

Using This Book *(For the professional)*

Why are some people excellent members of a team while others are unable to work effectively as members of a team? Over the last century many different workbooks, workshops, and self-help systems have been designed to help people develop teams, choose team members and work effectively as members of a team. In the past twenty years, many research studies have focused on the value of self-reflection and journaling as a way of exploring personal characteristics, identifying ineffective behaviors, and examining thoughts and feelings that lead to these ineffective behaviors. This book is unique in that it combines two powerful psychological tools for team building: self-assessment and journaling.

The Successful Team-Building Workbook contains five separate sections that will help participants learn more about themselves, as well as how prepared they are, to be effective team members:

Team Player Scale helps individuals determine how effective they will be in working with other people as part of a team.

Team Roles Scale helps individuals identify the skills they possess and how these skills affect the role or roles they will play as part of a team.

Team Personality Scale helps individuals identify their personality types and allows team leaders to harmonize personality types for effective team collaboration.

Team Leader Scale helps individuals explore how successful they would be in being a leader of a team.

Team Communicator Scale helps individuals identify how effective they are in sending feedback to team members and receiving feedback from team members.

These sections serve as avenues for individual self-reflection, as well as for group experiences revolving around identified topics of importance. Each assessment includes directions for easy administration, scoring and interpretation. Each section includes exploratory activities, reflective journaling exercises and educational handouts to help participants discover their habitual, ineffective efforts working as part of a team, and explore new ways to contribute to team success.

The art of self-reflection goes back many centuries and is rooted in many of the world's greatest spiritual and philosophical traditions. Socrates, the ancient Greek philosopher, was known to walk the streets engaging the people he met in philosophical reflection and dialogue. He felt that this type of activity was so important in life that he went so far as to proclaim, "The unexamined life is not worth living!" The unexamined life is one in which the same routine is continually repeated without ever thinking about its meaning to one's life and how this life really could be lived. However, a structured reflection and examination of beliefs, assumptions, characteristics and patterns can provide a better understanding which

Using This Book *(For the professional, continued)*

can lead to a more satisfying life and career. A greater level of self-understanding about important life skills is often necessary to make positive, self-directed changes in the negative patterns that keep repeating throughout life. The assessments and exercises in this book can help promote this self-understanding.

Through involvement in the in-depth activities, the participant claims ownership in the development of positive patterns.

Journaling is an extremely powerful tool for enhancing self-discovery, learning, transcending traditional problems, breaking ineffective life and career habits, and helping to heal from psychological traumas of the past. From a physical point of view, writing reduces stress and lowers muscle tension, blood pressure and heart rate levels. Psychologically, writing reduces sadness, depression and general anxiety, and leads to a greater level of life satisfaction and optimism. Behaviorally, writing leads to enhanced social skills, emotional intelligence and creativity.

By combining reflective assessment and journaling, your participants will engage in a revolutionary method for ensuring team success.

Preparation for using the assessments and activities in this book is important. The authors suggest that prior to administering any of the assessments in this book, you complete them yourself. This will familiarize you with the format of the assessments, the scoring directions, the interpretation guides and the journaling activities. Although the assessments are designed to be self-administered, scored and interpreted, it helps for facilitators to be prepared to answer questions about the assessments for participants.

With your background and experience, as well as familiarity with the tests, you should be able to clarify for participants any confusing words or phrases.

Thanks to the following professionals whose input in this book has been invaluable!

Kathy Khalsa, OTR/L

Jay Leutenberg

Kathy Liptak, Ed.D.

Eileen Regen, M.Ed., CJE

The Assessments, Journaling Activities, and Educational Handouts

The Assessments, Journaling Activities, and Educational Handouts sections in *The Successful Team-Building Workbook* are reproducible and ready to be photocopied for participants' use. Assessments contained in this book focus on self-reported data and are similar to ones used by psychologists, counselors, therapists and career consultants. Accuracy and usefulness of the information provided is dependent on the truthful information that each participant provides through self-examination. By being honest, participants help themselves to learn about unproductive and ineffective patterns, and to uncover information that might be keeping them from being as content and/or as successful as they might be.

An assessment instrument can provide participants with valuable information about themselves; however, it cannot measure or identify everything about them. The assessments' purposes are not to pigeon-hole certain characteristics, but rather to allow participants to explore all of their characteristics. This book contains self-assessments, not tests. Tests measure knowledge or whether something is right or wrong. For the assessments in this book, there are no right or wrong answers. These assessments ask for personal opinions or attitudes about a topic of importance in the participant's career and life.

When administering assessments in this workbook, remember that the items are generically written so that they will be applicable to a wide variety of people but will not account for every possible variable for every person. The assessments are not specifically tailored to one person. Use them to help participants identify negative themes in their lives and find ways to break the hold that these patterns and their effects have in their life and career.

Advise the participants taking the assessments that they should not spend too much time trying to analyze the content of the questions; their initial response will most likely be true. Regardless of individual scores, encourage participants to talk about their findings and their feelings pertaining to what they have discovered about themselves. Talking about and exploring team-building exercises can be helpful to the participants now and for the rest of their lives. These team-building exercises will be beneficial in their future.

Layout of the Book

The Successful Team-Building Workbook is designed to be used either independently or as part of an integrated curriculum. You may administer one of the assessments and the journaling exercises to an individual or a group with whom you are working, or you may administer a number of the assessments over one or more days.

This book includes the following reproducibles in all 5 sections:

- **Assessment Instruments** – Self-assessment inventories with scoring directions and interpretation materials. Group facilitators can choose one or more of the activities relevant to their participants.
- **Activity Handouts** – Practical questions and activities that prompt self-reflection and promote self-understanding. These questions and activities foster introspection and promote pro-social behaviors.
- **Reflective Questions for Journaling** – Self-exploration activities and journaling exercises specific to each assessment to enhance self-discovery, learning, and healing.
- **Educational Handouts** – Handouts designed to enhance instruction can be used individually or in groups to promote a positive understanding of anger and to provide positive reinforcement for effective anger management. They can be distributed, converted into masters for overheads or transparencies, or written on a board and discussed.

Who should use this program?

This book has been designed as a practical tool for helping professionals, such as human resource managers, training specialists, outplacement counselors, career counselors, therapists, psychologists, teachers, group leaders, management teams, etc. Depending on the role of the professional using *The Successful Team-Building Workbook* and the specific group's needs, these sections can be used individually, combined or as part of an integrated curriculum, for a more comprehensive approach.

Why use self-assessments?

Self-assessments are important in teaching various team-building skills because they help participants to engage in these ways:

- Become aware of the primary motivators that guide their behavior.
- Explore and learn to let go of troublesome habits and behavioral patterns learned in childhood.
- Explore the effects of unconscious childhood messages.
- Gain insight and a wake-up call for behavioral change.
- Focus thinking on behavioral goals for change.
- Uncover resources they possess that can help them to cope better with problems and difficulties.
- Explore their personal characteristics without judgment.
- Develop full awareness of their strengths and weaknesses.

Because the assessments are presented in a straightforward and easy-to-use format, individuals can self-administer, score, and interpret each assessment at their own pace.

Introduction for the Participant

All people soon realize that they are on one or many teams in life.

Teams can be found in a variety of settings:

- Work
- Home
- Community
- Schools
- Athletic organizations

People are increasingly being asked, or choosing, to be members of teams. Teams are effective because they can simply accomplish more than any individual can. Teams are also effective because they allow for multiple perspectives on how to accomplish a goal or meet a particular need, utilize people with diverse skill sets, and integrate the strengths of people with different personality types. However, because members of a team are often very different, they must learn to work collaboratively and effectively in order to accomplish the team goals. This process is called team building.

Team building refers to a process of establishing and developing a sense of collaboration, open communication, and trust among team members. Teams or team members require people to have an interest in the goals of the team, be comfortable with the role as a member of the team, be able to harmonize with the personality types of other members of the team, learn to work collaboratively with others, support other's efforts, make effective use of team resources, and communicate effectively. Let's face it, being an effective member of a team, regardless of the type of team and the setting in which the team operates, requires a great deal of knowledge about the team process and about one's own personal qualities.

Effective team building requires that each member of the team recognize personal unique strengths and weaknesses, better understand the unique strengths and weaknesses of other team members, and learn skills for building, maintaining, and motivating a cohesive team. *The Successful Team-Building Workbook* is designed to help people learn more about themselves, discover how effectively they might function as part of a team, and explore ways of becoming better team members.

The Successful Team-Building Workbook

TABLE OF CONTENTS

TABLE OF CONTENTS

SECTION I:

Team Player Scale

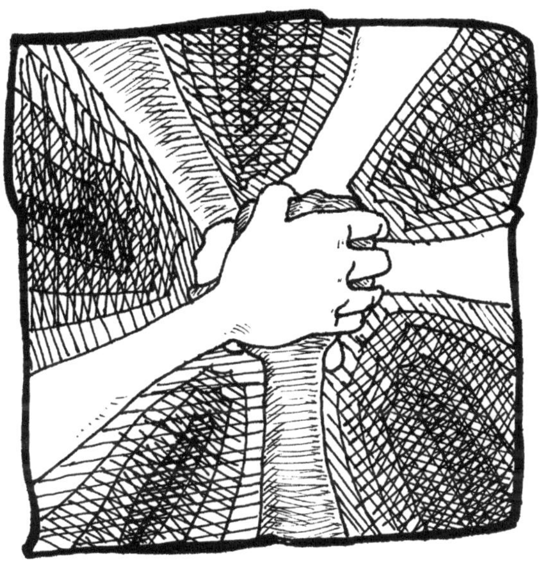

Name____

Date_________________________

Team Player Scale Directions

The Team Player Scale can help you determine how effective you will be in working with other people as part of a team. This assessment contains thirty-six statements. Read each statement and decide whether or not the statement describes you. In each of the choices listed, circle the number of your response on the line to the right of each statement.

4 = Very Much Like Me	3 = Usually Like Me	2 = Somewhat Like Me	1 = Not Like Me

In the following example, the circled 2 indicates the statement is somewhat like the person completing the assessment:

When I am working as part of a team, I . . .

1. welcome constructive criticism from others . . . 4 3 (2) 1

This is not a test and there are no right or wrong answers. Do not spend too much time thinking about your answers. Your initial response will likely be the most true for you. Be sure to respond to every statement.

(Turn to the next page and begin)

Team Player Scale

When I am working as part of a team, I . . .

	4 = Very Much Like Me	3 = Usually Like Me	2 = Somewhat Like Me	1 = Not Like Me
1. welcome constructive criticism from others	4	3	2	1
2. attend all meetings on time	4	3	2	1
3. am willing to help other group members	4	3	2	1
4. am open to differences in others	4	3	2	1
5. communicate ideas clearly	4	3	2	1
6. am prepared to work with team members	4	3	2	1
7. foster team spirit	4	3	2	1
8. will see others' points of view	4	3	2	1
9. communicate in a non-judgmental manner	4	3	2	1
10. keep the commitments I make to team members	4	3	2	1
11. show appreciation to members for their contributions	4	3	2	1
12. encourage differing opinions	4	3	2	1
13. ask questions and encourage others to do so	4	3	2	1
14. make team goals a priority	4	3	2	1
15. share new information openly with other team members	4	3	2	1
16. recognize the positive ideas of others	4	3	2	1
17. disagree with others in a tactful manner	4	3	2	1
18. maintain ethical standards in completing tasks	4	3	2	1

(Continued on the next page)

(Team Player Scale continued)

When I am working as part of a team, I . . .

	4 = Very Much Like Me	3 = Usually Like Me	2 = Somewhat Like Me	1 = Not Like Me
19. trust other members of the team to complete their tasks	4	3	2	1
20. am open to others' opinions	4	3	2	1
21. offer constructive feedback for others.	4	3	2	1
22. identify and respond to needs without being asked.	4	3	2	1
23. foster cooperation among other team members	4	3	2	1
24. am willing to change my mind	4	3	2	1
25. listen attentively to others	4	3	2	1
26. maintain the rules and practices of the team	4	3	2	1
27. foster participation among uncommitted team members	4	3	2	1
28. enjoy working with people different from me	4	3	2	1
29. make note of nonverbal and verbal cues and respond effectively	4	3	2	1
30. complete tasks efficiently.	4	3	2	1
31. am cooperative with others	4	3	2	1
32. respect the boundaries of others	4	3	2	1
33. confirm the contributions of other team members	4	3	2	1
34. am accountable for completing assigned tasks	4	3	2	1
35. coordinate my work with that of other team members	4	3	2	1
36. see possibilities in the differences of others.	4	3	2	1

(Go to the Scoring Directions on the next page)

Team Player Scale Scoring Directions

The Team Player Scale is designed to measure your ability to function as part of a team. Four areas have been identified to make up the components for the Team Player Scale:

Communication
Commitment
Cooperation
Connection

The items that comprise each of the four components are grouped in a way that will help you explore how you function as part of a team.

To score your assessment:

1. Record each of the scores from the previous two pages on the lines below. For example, if you circled the 4 for item number 1, you would put a 4 on the line above the 1 on the chart below. Do the same for all 36 items.

2. Add the totals for each of the 4 rows and put that total on the total line to the right.

___	___	___	___	___	___	___	___	___	______
1	5	9	13	17	21	25	29	33	Communication Total
___	___	___	___	___	___	___	___	___	______
2	6	10	14	18	22	26	30	34	Commitment Total
___	___	___	___	___	___	___	___	___	______
3	7	11	15	19	23	27	31	35	Cooperation Total
___	___	___	___	___	___	___	___	___	______
4	8	12	16	20	24	28	32	36	Connection Total

(The Profile Interpretation on the next page will help you interpret your scores)

Profile Interpretation of the Team Player Scale

Total Scale Scores	Result	Indications
Scores from 28 to 36	high	**High Scores** suggest that you are probably a great team member. You will function effectively as a team member.
Scores from 19 to 25	average	**Average Scores** suggest that you can be somewhat effective. You probably will function well as a team member.
Scores from 11 to 18	low	**Low Scores** suggest that this area is probably not one of your strengths. You probably will have difficulty functioning as a team member because of it.

The remainder of the assessment contains interpretation materials to help determine if you have the qualities of a productive team member. This scale can help you identify whether your strengths as a team member take the form of communication, commitment, cooperation and/or connection. The following sections will provide a description of the four critical components needed by team members as well as some self-reflective questions to help you enhance your team-building skills.

COMMUNICATION – People with high scores in this area tend to communicate well as a group member. They talk effectively with other team members and listen attentively to what other team members say. They let other team members know how they are progressing and use their communication skills to learn about the progress of their team members. They communicate ideas in a clear and non-judgmental manner. They are not afraid to ask questions and encourage other members of the group to do so. They show a great deal of empathy in being able to understand the verbal and non-verbal cues of other team members.

COMMITMENT – People with high scores in this area tend to be very committed to the goals of the team and the members of the team. They faithfully attend all team meetings and show up prepared to work toward team goals. They keep their commitments because team goals are their priority. They are intuitive about what needs to be accomplished to meet the team's goals and they work tirelessly to accomplish these tasks. They complete the tasks that are assigned and are accountable for the results of their assignments.

COOPERATION – People with high scores in this area are willing to help other team members achieve the tasks they are assigned. They do everything they can to enhance team spirit and acknowledge the accomplishments of other team members. They trust team members to accomplish their tasks and enjoy cooperation among team members. They will work with uncommitted team members to foster participation and will ensure that their work does not hamper the involvement of other team members.

CONNECTION – People with high scores in this area enjoy working with people who are different from themselves. They feel connected to the other members of the team because they can see all of the possibilities that diverse team members bring to the team goal. By looking at, and accepting, the strengths and weaknesses of other team members, they operate from a positive, optimistic point of view. They are open and willing to use suggestions by other team members. They believe that the differences in team members will enhance team performance. They are open to different points of view and encourage other team members to express their opinions.

Communication

For the exercises below, you may provide answers based on a current team of which you are a part, or you may provide answers about a team of which you will be a member in the future.

What communication challenges does your team have?

What are the communication strengths of your team?

What are the communication weaknesses of your team?

How can your team use communication to build trust?

How can open communication help your team?

Commitment

What does commitment mean to you?

____

____

____

What commitments are you willing to make to the team?

____

____

____

What situations in your life may affect your commitment to the team?

____

____

____

What doubts do you have about being able to commit to the team?

____

____

____

What concerns do you have about committing to the team?

____

____

____

Cooperation

How can a collaborative environment be established for the team?

How can the team ensure that information is passed collaboratively among team members?

How can the team ensure that open communication and sharing of idea occurs through the process?

How can members of the team work with members they do not like?

How can members of the team work with members they do not respect?

Connection

How do you use the differences of the members of your team to the benefit of the team?

How will the team-members' differences impact the team?

How will the differences of your team members hurt the progress to your goals?

How can members connect if they do not appreciate differences in others?

How can members connect with others who do not respect differences in others?

My Team — Positive Characteristics

In the spaces below, list the members of your team and any positive characteristics they might have to help the team reach its goals. You may provide answers based on a current team of which you are a part, or you may provide answers about a team of which you will be a member in the future.

TEAM MEMBER	POSITIVE CHARACTERISTICS
Jack	*Jack is passionate about his work and likes to share that enthusiasm with the rest of the team. He is always glad to listen to other team members' ideas.*

My Team — Negative Characteristics

In the spaces below list the members of your team and any negative characteristics they might use to hurt the team from reaching its goals.

TEAM MEMBER	NEGATIVE CHARACTERISTICS
Jack	*During a project, Jack does not always share his ideas with the rest of the team until he is finished working on his part.*

My Team History

Describe some of the teams on which you have worked in the past.

Were they successful or not? Why?

What roles did you play on these teams?

What team skills do you possess?

What team skills do you need to develop further?

What steps will you take to improve these skills?

Team Game Plan

Situation:

Team Goal:

Leader:

Team Members:

Strengths of the team:

Weaknesses of the team:

(Continued on the next page)

(Team Game Plan continued)

Needed Resources: ______________________________

____

____

____

Challenges of the team:

____

____

____

Actions to be taken:

____

____

____

____

____

____

____

____

____

____

____

____

Model Team

Describe how members of a model team can use communication to meet their goal.

How is this different from that of your actual team?

Expectations

When expectations are defined for a team, members of the team function more effectively. What are the expectations for your team?

Overall Vision

Describe what you see as the overall vision for your team.

What are some goals, desired outcomes and challenges of the team?

4 C's of a Team

- **COMMUNICATION** – The ability to communicate well as a member of a group, talk effectively with other team members and listen attentively to what other team members say.

- **COMMITMENT** – The ability to be very committed to the goals of the team and the members of the team, faithfully attend all team meetings and show up prepared to work toward team goals.

- **COOPERATION** – The ability to help other team members achieve the tasks they are assigned, enhance team spirit and acknowledge the accomplishments of other team members.

- **CONNECTION** – The ability to work with people who are different from you and connect to the other members of the team because of all of the possibilities that diverse team members bring to the team goal.

Stages in Team Building

- Develop a vision with goals and desired outcomes

- Encourage team members to agree to commit to the team vision

- Build trust among team members

- Find ways to include all members

- Establish an environment in which team members will collaborate to achieve the team vision

SECTION II:

Team Roles Scale

Name_______________________________________

Date_______________________

Team Roles Scale Directions

The Team Roles Scale can help you explore the skills that you bring to any team and how these skills help to determine the role or roles you will play as a part of the team. This assessment contains 44 skills statements. Read each of the statements and decide how much you agree. In each of the choices listed, circle the number of your response on the line to the right of each statement.

In the following example, the circled 1 indicates that the statement is not true of the person completing the scale:

When working as part of a team . . .

	Very True	**Somewhat True**	**Not True**
1. I work best in orderly, organized environment	3	2	(1)

This is not a test. Since there are no right or wrong answers, do not spend too much time thinking about your answers. Your initial response will likely be the most true for you. Be sure to respond to every statement.

(Turn to the next page and begin)

Team Roles Scale

When working as part of a team . . .	Very True	Somewhat True	Not True
1. I work best in orderly, organized environments	3	2	1
2. I am upbeat and optimistic, even when problems arise	3	2	1
3. I value intelligence in myself and in others	3	2	1
4. I respond to others with understanding and empathy	3	2	1
5. I take notes, and make sure meetings are focused	3	2	1
6. I help to keep team spirits up	3	2	1
7. I am analytic and insightful	3	2	1
8. I always listen to everyone's point of view before deciding	3	2	1
9. I am responsible and hard-working	3	2	1
10. I motivate other people to perform their best	3	2	1
11. I like to work and make decisions on my own	3	2	1
12. I invest a lot of emotion and time in my relationships	3	2	1
13. I take personal commitments very seriously	3	2	1
14. I like encouraging other people	3	2	1
15. I use logic and objectivity	3	2	1
16. I enjoy harmony and dislike conflict	3	2	1
17. I immediately begin planning the work of the group	3	2	1
18. Team spirit is the most critical aspect of a team	3	2	1
19. I prefer solitary assignments to team assignments	3	2	1
20. I like to understand and express my deepest feelings	3	2	1
21. I mostly communicate about concrete, observable information	3	2	1
22. I like keeping a high level of energy in the group	3	2	1

(Continued on the next page)

(Team Player Scale continued)

When working as part of a team . . .	**Very True**	**Somewhat True**	**Not True**
23. I tend to be skeptical	3	2	1
24. I tend to take things very personally	3	2	1
25. I enjoy coordinating	3	2	1
26. Other people say I am enthusiastic	3	2	1
27. I am good at analysis and problem solving	3	2	1
28. I usually help other people complete their tasks	3	2	1
29. I try to keep people focused on completing tasks	3	2	1
30. I like to get everyone excited about the task	3	2	1
31. I am good at staying objective and asking difficult questions	3	2	1
32. I take it on myself to ensure no conflicts arise	3	2	1
33. I double-check facts before presenting them	3	2	1
34. I attempt to keep conversations positive	3	2	1
35. I understand and see patterns in complex information	3	2	1
36. I am idealistic about group goals and tasks	3	2	1
37. I am accurate and detail-oriented	3	2	1
38. I encourage people to participate in discussions	3	2	1
39. I like to ask questions	3	2	1
40. I make sure that nobody is left out of discussions	3	2	1
41. I keep track of the progress of others	3	2	1
42. I find group work to be exciting and fun	3	2	1
43. I connect more with others' minds than their hearts	3	2	1
44. I am a good listener	3	2	1

(Go to the Scoring Directions on the next page)

Team Roles Scale Scoring

The roles that you play when you are part of a team are defined by how you behave and interact with other members of the team. Your skill set will largely define the roles that you play within a team. The important thing to remember is that no role is more important than any other and that each role has its own strengths and weaknesses. People who are part of a team play one or more of the four roles that are measured with this assessment. These roles make up the four scales on the assessment. Scales are used to group items and help you to explore your specific roles on a part of any team. After you determine your scores and identify the specific scale on which you scored highest, there will be an in-depth profile of each role.

Scoring the assessment is a very easy process. Look at the questions you just answered. Use the spaces below to record the number that you circled on each individual item of the assessment. Then calculate the totals for each of the columns (scales) and put that total underneath each column.

SCALE 1	SCALE 2	SCALE 3	SCALE 4
1 ______	2 ______	3 ______	4 ______
5 ______	6 ______	7 ______	8 ______
9 ______	10 ______	11 ______	12 ______
13 ______	14 ______	15 ______	16 ______
17 ______	18 ______	19 ______	20 ______
21 ______	22 ______	23 ______	24 ______
25 ______	26 ______	27 ______	28 ______
29 ______	30 ______	31 ______	32 ______
33 ______	34 ______	35 ______	36 ______
37 ______	38 ______	39 ______	40 ______
41 ______	42 ______	43 ______	44 ______
I. Total	II. Total	III. Total	IV. Total
______	______	______	______
Organizer	**Motivator**	**Analyzer**	**Listener**

Team Roles Scale

By learning more about your assigned roles on a team, it will help you to know your place as part of the team. Team members are usually assigned roles based on skills they possess. It is important to clarify each of the different roles so that team members know exactly what it is that they have to do. Most of the time, the team leader must rely on intuition and prior relationships in assigning roles. The purpose of this assessment is to provide you and your team leaders and you with information about what might be your best role as part of a team.

Look at the profile interpretation materials below. The area in which you scored the highest tends to be the role you would perform best as part of the team. Similarly, the area in which you scored the lowest tends to be the role you would not perform well, as part of the team. Remember that if roles are assigned to account for your strengths, the effectiveness of the team will be enhanced.

Profile Interpretation

Total Scale Scores	Result	Indications
Scores from 26 to 33	high	**A high score** means that the role represented by this scale very closely matches your skill set. You will probably function effectively in this role as a part of any team.
Scores from 19 to 25	moderate	**A moderate score** means that the role represented by this scale somewhat closely matches your skill set. You are able to perform this role as a part of any team, but you may not always function effectively.
Scores from 11 to 18	low	**A low score** means that the role represented by this scale does not match your skill set. You probably do not function effectively in this role as a part of any team.

For scales in which you scored in the **Moderate** or **High** range, find the descriptions on the four team roles on the pages that follow. Then, read the description and complete the exercises that are included. No matter how you scored, low, moderate or high, you will benefit from all of these exercises.

Team Roles Scale – Organizer

Your role as part of any team is one of organizing the team members, the process, and the project. You are a person with a plan, and one who always needs to have a plan to function. You make your way in the business world by reaching one goal, another and then another. You are very good at organizing your thoughts and planning what you say. You tend to be somewhat rigid in your thinking and often are not open to the views of other people. In your head, you have a giant "to-do list" where you keep track of projects you have to complete. Then, as you complete a project, you take it off your list and add a new one to it. You enjoy working in orderly, structured environments where you can organize the people and the work in your head. You set long-range goals and want to do only those things that suit your purpose. Your mind thinks in such an orderly fashion that you see figures, charts, and graphs. For you, organizing is an essential part of your life. You cannot function in a messy workplace or with a messy team. You must have things organized or you cannot function.

AS A TEAM MEMBER:

Given your skills, what do you see as an effective role for you as part of any team?

____

____

____

____

Given your skills, what do you think are your strengths and weaknesses?

____

____

____

____

(Continued on the next page)

(Team Roles Scale – Organizer continued)

You are a master planner. Describe times when your need for a plan has hurt you and the teams of which you have been a part.

You love planning every detail. Describe a time when you were so worried about the details that you slowed up the progress of the team.

You like everything planned in advance. How could you start being more spontaneous in your role as a team member?

Team Roles Scale – Motivator

You enjoy communicating in an action-oriented, hands-on environment that stimulates your senses. You tend to take what people say literally and at face value. You tend to communicate with an easy, informal style that people enjoy. Your language tends to be uncomplicated and down-to-earth. You have lots of energy and get frustrated when trapped in a long conversation. You are open-minded about the types of conversation topics you entertain. You are often unavailable to sit down for quiet conversation times. You love situations that are unpredictable and allow you to be spontaneous. You tend to be the life of the party in social situations. You love being around other people and tend to attract people like a magnet. You can become silly if you become too spontaneous.

AS A TEAM MEMBER:

Given your skill set, what do you see as an effective role for you as part of any team?

____

____

____

____

Given your skill set, what do you think are your strengths and weaknesses?

____

____

____

____

(Continued on the next page)

(Team Roles Scale – Motivator continued)

You are a master motivator. Describe times when your motivation style has hurt you and hurt teams you have been a part of in the past.

____

____

____

____

You are skilled at motivating yourself and other team members. Describe a time and a team where you were unable to motivate other team members.

____

____

____

____

You tend to have a high level of energy. How has this energy level help you and hurt you?

____

____

____

____

Team Roles Scale – Analyzer

You let emotions, ego and/or impulse get in your way. You let numbers, facts and/or logic take the lead, and then approach challenges and problems with cool detachment. You like structure, preferably in the form of outlines and business plans. You prefer thinking about and talking about concrete, tangible, observable information. When you are communicating with team members, you like it when things are stated clearly and make sense to you. You enjoy specifics that you can look at analytically. You do not like things that are abstract or require you to search for hidden meanings. When the team begins to talk about theoretical concepts or abstract ideas, you get them back on track. You enjoy gathering and using information in a practical way. You prefer brief interactions that get straight to the point. You are detail-oriented, focused and very analytical in your communication with others.

AS A TEAM MEMBER:

Given your skill set, what do you see as an effective role for you as part of any team?

____

____

____

____

Given your skill set, what do you think are your strengths and weaknesses?

____

____

____

____

(Continued on the next page)

(Team Roles Scale – Analyzer continued)

Sometimes you can be silent, cool or resistant in social situations. How can you overcome this behavior?

____

____

____

____

Describe times when your constant analysis has hurt you and hurt the teams you have been a part of in the past.

____

____

____

____

You are always objective and level-headed. What are some situations where these attributes might work against you?

____

____

____

____

Team Roles Scale - Listener

As a member of any team, you are very easy to get along with. You are so inoffensive and pleasant to be around that you are a very valuable asset to any team. Your low-key personality seems to bring all team members and problems into perspective. You don't like to think too far ahead and you will take things as they come. You have the ability to stay calm regardless of what is happening with the team. You do not seem to be in a hurry and you do not get disturbed over matters that would bother others. You are a great listener and mediator of problems. You like to keep peace among other team members. As others begin to fight or disagree, you have the ability to sit back and give an objective opinion. You unique gift is the ability to win friends and influence team members because you are so easy to get along with. You would rather listen to others than talk yourself. You are very sensitive to subtle nuances in communication such as a person's body language, facial expressions and vocal intonations. You tend to be very good at reading between the lines, understanding empathetically what other people are saying and perceiving underlying meanings in others' words.

AS A TEAM MEMBER:

Given your skill set, what do you see as an effective role for you as a part of any team?

____

____

____

____

Given your skill set, what do you think are your strengths and weaknesses?

____

____

____

____

(Continued on the next page)

(Team Roles Scale – Listener continued)

You sit back and listen to others. Describe times when this quality has hurt you as well as the teams you have been a part of in the past.

You often provide a sympathetic ear to others. What can you do to get others to provide a sympathetic ear to you when the need arises?

You like to be a team mediator. How could this role actually hurt the team process?

(Continued on the next page)

Team Roles and Responsibilities

Team leader and team member roles and responsibilities need to be clearly defined at the outset of any team project. Fill in the spaces below to organize your team:

Team Leader: ______________________________

Role: ______________________________

Responsibilities: ______________________________

____

____

Team Member: ______________________________

Role: ______________________________

Responsibilities: ______________________________

____

____

Team Member: ______________________________

Role: ______________________________

Responsibilities: ______________________________

____

____

Team Member: ______________________________

Role: ______________________________

Responsibilities: ______________________________

____

____

Skills & Personality Characteristics

How can a team leader best use your skills and personality characteristics?

My Teams

Describe teams that you have been a part of in the past.

What roles did you play?

My Benefits

How did you benefit from being a member of the past team?

How will you benefit from being a member of a team in the future?

Advantages of a Team

- Teams involve multiple people, and incorporate many types of personalities, resources and ideas
- Teams are able to maximize the strengths of its members and minimize their weaknesses
- Teams build a sense of community
- Teams incorporate multiple perspectives to achieve their goals

Four Roles That Team Members Play

Organizer – *The person responsible for ensuring that the team has a plan and sticks to that plan.*

Motivator – *The person responsible for ensuring that the team stays motivated to accomplish their task.*

Analyzer – *The person responsible for using logic and objectivity in the problem-solving tasks of the team.*

Listener – *The person who is responsible for ensuring that team members support and respect each other and seek the help they need to complete their tasks.*

SECTION III:

Team Personality Scale

Name____

Date__________________________

Team Personality Scale Directions

One of the critical aspects in the success of any team is the ability of its members to get along with one another and work together. Because all people have different personality traits, this can be one of the biggest challenges for any team leader. The Team Personality Scale contains eighty words used to describe the many aspects of a personality. Read each of the words and decide whether the word describes you when you are making decisions. If the statement does describe you, circle the word in the column. If the statement *does not* describe you, *do not* circle the word, simply move to the next word.

In the following example, the circled words indicate that they are descriptive of the person completing the scale.

I am:

Spontaneous

Playful

Adventurous

Idea-centered

Artistic

This is not a test, and there are no right or wrong answers. Do not spend too much time thinking about your answers. Your initial response will likely be the most true for you. Be sure to respond to every word listed.

(Turn to the next page and begin)

Team Personality Scale

Circle only the words and phrases that *best* describe you:

I am:

Spontaneous	Logical	Planner	Patient
Playful	Systematic	Careful	Supportive
Adventurous	Accurate	Organized	Loyal
Idea-centered	Exact	Conservative	Warm
Artistic	Precise	Cautious	Calm
Musical	Diplomatic	Detailed	Predictable
Imaginative	Disciplined	Structured	Gentle
Flexible	Mathematical	Controlling	Considerate
Inspiring	Economical	Practical	Friendly
Visionary	Deepthinker	Orderly	Shy
Creative	Intellectual	Concrete	Goodlistener
Resourceful	Fact-oriented	Direct	Reserved
Intuitive	Realistic	Methodical	Tolerant
Risktaker	Investigating	Responsible	Even-tempered
Animated	Experimenting	Enjoysroutine	Attentive
Insightful	Technical	Thorough	People-oriented
Innovative	Objective	Independent	Goodnatured
Entertaining	Perfectionistic	Dependable	Compassionate
Inventive	Analytical	Down-to-earth	Nurturing
Curious	Decisive	Productive	Sensitive
TOTAL I _______	TOTAL II _______	TOTAL III _______	TOTAL IV _______

(Continued on the next page)

Team Personality Scale Scoring

The Team Personality Scale is designed to measure your personality traits so that you can better understand yourself as well as others on your team. For all of the items on the previous page, count the total number of items you circled for each column. Put that total on the line marked "Total" at the bottom of each of the four columns and then transfer your totals to the space below:

I. Innovative = ________

II. Realistic = ________

III. Detailed = ________

IV. Supportive = ________

Profile Interpretation

Total Scale Scores	Result	Indications
Scores from 14 to 20	high	You possess many of the personality characteristics of this personality type.
Scores from 7 to 13	moderate	You possess some of the personality characteristics of this personality type.
Scores from 0 to 6	low	You do not possess many of the personality characteristics of this personality type.

The area in which you scored the highest tends to be your most used team personality type. Similarly, the area in which you scored the lowest tends to be your least used team personality type. If time is limited, read only the information and answer the questions for the area in which you scored highest. If time permits, you can read about the other team personality types. Now turn to the next pages for descriptions of each of the four personality types on this scale.

I – Profile Interpretation – Innovative

Innovative personality types are generous, fun-loving and adventurous. They enjoy living their life here-and-now and rarely think about what will happen in the future. They value freedom and hate to feel controlled or obligated. They are spontaneous and trust their own impulses to help them make decisions. They live for a variety of experiences and feel competent in handling any situations that arise and recover easily from setbacks. They like to see the tangible results of their work and will take risks necessary to meet the challenges in their lives. They like to make their work as fun as possible, and they seek occupations that are exciting and have some associated adventure. They seek work as an opportunity to experience other aspects of their lives. They respond well to challenges and crises, but take immediate action and then quickly lose interest. They are great at solving immediate problems and then taking action to solve the problems. They do not like rules, routines or structured work environments. They like working with practical, action-oriented people.

List the ways your team personality type can help the team process.

____

____

____

List the ways your team personality type can hinder the team process.

____

____

____

What do you see as your primary role in the team process?

____

____

____

(Profile Interpretation continued on the next page)

II – Profile Interpretation – Realistic

Realistic personality types are innovative, inquisitive and analytical. They highly value competency and intellectual knowledge. They prize intelligence in themselves and others and want to constantly improve their base of knowledge. They strive to be able to understand and explain how the natural world works. To do so, they use their insight and intellect to create theories and models to develop better understanding of the world around them. They are adept at understanding and synthesizing complex information, and developing and focusing on long-range goals. They like developing, designing and building models for new ways of doing things and making things better. They are not very interested in the day-to-day details, but are more interested in self-mastery and in making a unique contribution in their area of specialization. They value independence and autonomy and can be argumentative and opinionated about things they believe in. They enjoy work environments with objective standards and offer opportunities to attain recognition from peers in their area of specialization.

List the ways your team personality type can help the team process.

List the ways your team personality type can hinder the team process.

What do you see as your primary role in the team process?

(Profile Interpretation continued on the next page)

III – Profile Interpretation – Detailed

Detailed personality types are realistic, practical and responsible in the way they do things. They like to be fully in charge of their specific responsibilities. They want to be valuable parts of any organization and will take on additional assignments to make a contribution. They feel like they must be the responsible one if the work is to be done. They have a strong work ethic and believe that hard work is the most important factor in being successful. They believe that they can achieve anything by simply working hard to achieve it. They serve and bring tremendous stability to any organization. They want their supervisors to judge their performance based on a specific set of job responsibilities. They do not like change, especially if they do not understand the reason for the change. They are reliable, hard-working and value common sense, not theories, vague information or abstract thinking.

List the ways your team personality type can help the team process.

____

____

____

List the ways your team personality type can hinder the team process.

____

____

____

What do you see as your primary role in the team process?

____

____

____

(Profile Interpretation continued on the next page)

IV – Profile Interpretation – Supportive

Supportive personality types are warm and compassionate and have a vision for what the ideal world looks like and then they work to create that world here on earth. They are optimistic and enjoy work that allows them to use their creativity and individuality to use their insight and helpful nature to benefit other people. They are interested in helping other people to realize their unique potential. They are sensitive to the needs of others and are skilled at bringing out the best in others. They like to be mentally stimulated and often come with new and interesting ideas and solutions to problems. They enjoy working in friendly, conflict-free environments where personal growth and development are encouraged by supervisors. They put a great deal of energy into projects and are easily disappointed when projects or people do not turn out as expected. They genuinely want to learn about, and better understand, themselves and others.

List the ways your team personality type can help the team process.

List the ways your team personality type can hinder the team process.

What do you see as your primary role in the team process?

Exploring Your Personality Type

It is important that you better understand the effects of your personality type on a team attempting to complete a task. Complete the following questions to learn more about you and your specific personality type:

What do you like most about your personality type?

____

____

____

What do you like least about your personality type?

____

____

____

How do others describe your personality?

____

____

____

What would you like to change about your personality?

____

____

____

(Continued on the next page)

(Exploring Your Personality Type, continued)

Is your personality similar to that of either of your parents? In what ways?

____

____

____

What types of personalities do you not get along with well? Why?

____

____

____

How does your personality impact team dynamics?

____

____

____

Given your team personality type, how would you describe your communication style?

____

____

____

How does your personality type complement other personality types?

____

____

____

Identify Personality Types

Personality types are observable in all lifestyles. Given the four different type of team personality types identified with the assessment – **Innovative**, **Realistic**, **Detailed** and **Supportive** – try to identify the personality type of the people listed in the first column. In the second column, list the personality type of the person defined. Then in the third column, list the reasons why you think he or she is that particular type.

PERSON	PERSONALITY TYPE	WHY?
Police Officer		
Manager		
Counselor		
Teacher		
Accountant		
Marketing Agent		
Social Worker		

Positive Personality Types

It is critical that team leaders and team members are able to recognize different personality types in their organization and then use these personality types to make their team more effective and successful. Your team is, or will be, comprised of many different personality types. In each of the spaces below, list each of the members of a current team or list the members of a team of which you will be a member in the future. Then, identify their *positive* personality characteristics.

TEAM MEMBER	POSITIVE PERSONALITY CHARACTERISTICS

Negative Personality Traits

It is critical that team leaders and team members are able to recognize different personality types in their organization and then use these personality types to make their team more effective and successful. Your team is, or will be, comprised of many different personality types. In each of the spaces below, list each of the members of a current team or list the members of a team of which you will be a member in the future. Then, identify their *negative* personality characteristics.

TEAM MEMBER	NEGATIVE PERSONALITY CHARACTERISTICS

Your Dream Team

One of the most difficult jobs of a team leader is piecing together an effective team. Putting together the perfect team is a very difficult process because of the different personality types that people bring to the team. If you are in the process of forming a team, develop a list of your dream-team members and describe why you want them as part of your team. If you will be forming a team in the future, write about people that you would like to have on your team. If you will not be forming a team, pretend that you have been given an assignment to form a team and complete a task. Think about what your dream team would look like. These can be people with whom you currently work, people in your community (teacher, doctor, etc.), well known figures in popular culture (Donald Trump, Oprah Winfrey), or historical figures (Abraham Lincoln, Betsy Ross).

PROSPECTIVE TEAM MEMBER	WHY YOU WANT HIM / HER ON YOUR TEAM

Upcoming Team Task

Think about an upcoming task that will require you to be on a team. The following questions will help you to begin thinking about the type of team you will need:

1. What is the task the team will need to work on?

2. List the important information you need to gather in order to do the work as a team.

3. List the person whom you think should be the team leader? Why this person?

4. What other people would comprise the team? Why them?

5. What is the desired outcome for the team?

Helpful Work Personality Traits

Describe the aspects of your personality that you believe *help you most* in your work?

Not-So-Helpful Work Personality Traits

Describe the aspects of your personality that you believe *help you least* in your work?

Personality Traits I Want to Develop

What personality traits, in the three personality types different from yours, would you most like to have? Why?

Basic Ground Rules for Teams

1) **All team members attend team meetings.**

2) **All team members participate in discussions, without interrupting.**

3) **Information is confidential unless team members say otherwise.**

4) **All team members have input in decision making.**

5) **All team members have tasks and complete them.**

6) **Relationships among team members are consistently positive and rewarding.**

Suggestions for Team Success

- Know yourself and the other members of your team
- Understand the goal of the team
- Find your niche within the team
- Trust your team leader
- Look at the big picture for the team
- Understand your role as a part of the team
- Rely on your past successes
- Be tolerant of different work styles and personality types

SECTION IV:

Team Leader Scale

Name____

Date________________________

Team Leader Scale Directions

In today's society, teams are rapidly becoming the way that people complete tasks and reach goals. Teams provide a venue for accomplishing tasks that probably could not be accomplished as well by one person alone. To be an effective leader you need to be able to communicate, foster collaboration, inspire and motivate others and manage the team-building process. This Team Leader Scale was designed to help you examine if you have the qualities to be or become a great leader of teams.

This assessment contains 40 statements that are representative of the qualities of effective team leaders. Read each of the statements and decide whether the statement describes you. If the statement is TRUE, circle the number next to that item under the TRUE column. If the statement is FALSE, circle the number next to that item under the FALSE column.

In the following example, the circled number under FALSE indicates the statement is not true of the person completing the scale.

	TRUE	FALSE
(A) I can get my point across effectively	2	(1)

This is not a test. Since there are no right or wrong answers, do not spend too much time thinking about your answers. Your initial response will likely be the most true for you. Be sure to respond to every statement.

(Turn to the next page and begin)

Team Leader Scale

	TRUE	FALSE
(A) I get my point across effectively	2	1
(A) I focus on the process, not on the person, when giving constructive criticism.	2	1
(A) I give feedback that builds, rather than destroys others	2	1
(A) I know when to use humor to relieve tension	2	1
(A) I single people out when they are nonproductive	1	2
(A) I communicate well as a leader	2	1
(A) I am good at asking for input and listening to my team members	2	1
(A) I don't handle group conflicts well	2	1
(A) I communicate my feelings as well as my ideas	2	1
(A) I clearly define tasks that need to be completed	2	1
(B) I am able to see possibilities for team success	2	1
(B) I imagine opportunities for the team members	2	1
(B) I have trouble adapting to diverse work styles	2	1
(B) I nurture a climate that promotes mutual trust	2	1
(B) I instill a culture of respect	2	1
(B) I create a context for risk-taking by team members	2	1
(B) I find it hard to build a strong team identity	2	1
(B) I create and maintain team direction	2	1
(B) I harness the power of team collaboration	2	1
(B) I help develop positive relationships among the team	2	1

(Continued on the next page)

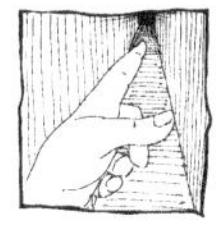

(Team Leader Scale, continued)

	TRUE	FALSE
(C) I foster enthusiasm in others because I'm enthusiastic	2	1
(C) I inspire people to share my vision for the team	2	1
(C) I get the team's participation in the project	2	1
(C) I help others feel a sense of ownership	2	1
(C) I work to help members feel committed to the team	2	1
(C) I have trouble empowering other people	1	2
(C) I am good at building team synergy	2	1
(C) I inspire a diverse team to work together	2	1
(C) I don't feel like it's my job to encourage and inspire others	1	2
(C) I like to get to know, encourage and motivate others	2	1
(D) I don't have the skills of a born leader	1	2
(D) I detect when team members are ready for new challenges	2	1
(D) I am good at moving teams forward	2	1
(D) I have trouble holding people accountable	1	2
(D) I define and enforce team ground rules	2	1
(D) I easily identify team needs and resources	2	1
(D) I am not a great problem solver	1	2
(D) I take needed actions in difficult situations	2	1
(D) I hesitate making difficult decisions	1	2
(D) I delegate responsibilities to build team unity	2	1

(Go to the Scoring Directions on the next page)

Team Leader Scoring Directions

The Team Leader Scale is designed to measure how effective you will be as the leader of a team. To get your score, total the numbers that you circled for the statements marked (A) in the previous section. You will get a number from 10 to 20. Put that number in the space marked "(A) – Communication Total" below. Then do the same for the other three scales – (B) Collaboration, (C) Motivating Others, and (D) Task Management.

(A) – COMMUNICATION TOTAL = ________

(B) – COLLABORATION TOTAL = ________

(C) – MOTIVATING OTHERS TOTAL = ________

(D) – TASK MANAGEMENT TOTAL = ________

Profile Interpretation

Total Scale Scores	Result	Indications
Scores from 17 to 20	high	A high score indicates that you show the tendencies of an effective team leader on this scale.
Scores from 14 to 16	moderate	A moderate score indicates that you show some of the tendencies of an effective team leader on this scale.
Scores from 10 to 13	low	A low score indicates that you show few tendencies of an effective team leader on this scale.

Team Leader Scale Descriptions

A - COMMUNICATION

People scoring high in the Communication section know that creating an effective team requires communication among team members. They are aware that only with good communication can a team succeed. It does not matter whether their team is a family, company, ministry, ball club or youth group; they know that communication increases connection and commitment.

B - COLLABORATION

People scoring high in the Collaboration section realize that it is in no one's best interest to create competition among team members. They know that cooperation is much more likely to produce positive outcomes than competition. They are able to develop cooperative goals, sustain ongoing interactions among members, build trusting relationships, share information and resources, and listen to other team members.

C – MOTIVATING OTHERS

People scoring high in the Motivating Others section are able to inspire and motivate the team members to strive toward a common goal. They are able to effectively communicate their vision for the team and gain a commitment from team members. They recognize the contributions of team members and enable others to act. They foster renewed loyalty and commitment, and inspire team members to excel.

D – TASK MANAGEMENT

People scoring high in the Task Management section are able to understand the importance of building and maintaining the team structure. They understand the team's purpose and they are able to envision the final outcome. They have great teamwork skills including organizational abilities, problem-solving skills, preparation skills and they are able to hold team members accountable. They are able to take needed actions and make difficult decisions.

Regardless of the scores on the assessment, the following exercises have been designed to help all team leaders.

Increasing Your Leadership Ability

It can be challenging when diverse people are thrust together and are asked to work like a team in order to achieve a common goal. Team leaders must have a variety of different skills and be adept at the team-building process. This process will probably be different for all teams based on the people who comprise the team and the nature of the project. However, the process will flow through a variety of stages that include task managing, motivating other team members, developing collaboration among team members and enhancing communication among team members.

Task Management

One of the most important aspects in building any team is the selection of team participants. The team leader must be able to have a vision for the team and then select team members who can ensure the success of the project and that vision. The team members must have confidence in each other and be able to trust one another. To determine the team members who will help you to complete your project, fill in the worksheet below. One of the best ways to create an effective team is to balance people's skill sets or have experts from different fields as part of the team. Some member might utilize technical skills, theoretical skills, organizational skills or networking skills.

POTENTIAL TEAM MEMBER	HOW THE PERSON WILL CONTRIBUTE TO THE TEAM SUCCESS
1.	
2.	
3.	
4.	
5.	

Establishment of Team Goals and Rules

To be effective, teams must develop shared values and ground rules. This is determining a goal that can be achieved, the setting of ground rules, and establishing the team meeting process and schedule. Fill in the spaces below:

TEAM GOALS & RULES	SHARED RESPONSES
What is the major goal for the team?	
What is the attendance policy?	
How will discussions be handled?	
What are the confidentiality rules?	
How will decisions be made?	
How will confrontation be handled?	
How will the team stay on task?	
When, and for how long, will the team meet?	
What will you want to accomplish during team meetings?	

Allocation of Team Roles

Based on the skills of the members of the team, use the spaces below to assign roles to team members so that they know their place on the team. These roles should be assigned based on each person's talents and skills.

TEAM MEMBER 1	TEAM MEMBER 2	TEAM MEMBER 3	TEAM MEMBER 4	TEAM MEMBER 5

Develop Collaboration Among Team Members

Developing cooperative goals is probably the best way to begin developing collaboration among team members. The best way to develop collaboration among team members is by developing cooperative goals and building trust. Think about your final team goal and sub-goals for your project. Then, fill in the spaces below:

Final Team Goal or Outcome: ______________________________

____

____

Sub-goal #1

Sub-goal #2

Sub-goal #3

Sub-goal #4

Sub-goal #5

Trust

Trust is at the heart of fostering collaboration among team members. It is the primary issue that allows team members to communicate effectively as team members. Team leaders who build trust are willing to consider alternative viewpoints and use people's skills and abilities to the fullest.

What happens when you do not trust the team leader?

What happens when you do not trust other team members?

How do you know when to trust team members?

Motivation

Motivating others involves believing in others and inspiring them. Team leaders can motivate others by helping them to buy into the leader's vision for the task at hand and allowing them to feel ownership for their part as a team member. Team leaders can motivate team members by putting them in positions where they can succeed on the team by communicating effectively and succinctly and by remaining detail-oriented in managing the tasks of the team.

WHY TEAMS NEED MOTIVATION	HOW I WILL ACCOMPLISH THE TASK
To take calculated risks	
To increase choice and decision-making	
To accept more responsibility	
To believe in other members of the team	
To increase interactions among team members	
To complete assigned tasks	
To get team members to take action	
To celebrate their accomplishments	
To envision the future	

Enhance Communication Among Team Members

Communication among team members can take many forms including nonverbal expressions and body language, negotiation, conflict management, decision making and day-to-day interactions. The need for clear and concise interactions among team members can mean the difference between a successful outcome and an unsuccessful outcome. Answer the following questions to help determine how your team is communicating:

Why do you think it is important for teams to have good communication?

____

____

____

____

____

How do leader(s) on your team communicate with other members of the team?

____

____

____

____

____

Do team leader(s) communicate with clear, consistent and courteous messages?

____

____

____

____

____

(Continued on the next page)

(Enhance Communication Among Team Members, continued)

How is communication uniting or breaking your team apart?

____

____

____

____

____

____

How can members of the team improve their communication?

____

____

____

____

____

____

What can you do to help build trust and open communication among team members?

____

____

____

____

____

____

Leadership Skills

What leadership skills do you wish you possessed?

How can you attain additional skills?

Leadership Style

How would you describe your leadership style?

Is that leadership style working for you? Why or why not?

Taking More Responsibility

How will you begin to take more responsibility for your own leadership growth?

The Power of a Team

This fall, when you see geese heading south for the winter flying along in the "V" formation, you might consider what science has discovered as to why they fly that way.

FACT: As each bird flaps its wings, it creates an "uplift" for the bird immediately following. By flying in the "V" formation, the whole flock has at least 71% greater flying range than if each bird flew on its own.
LESSON: People who share a common direction and sense of community can get where they are going more quickly and easily because they are traveling on the thrust of one another.

FACT: When a goose flies out of formation, it suddenly feels the drag and resistance of trying to go it alone. It quickly gets back into formation to take advantage of the lifting power of the bird in front of it.
LESSON: If we have as much common sense as a goose, we stay in formation with those headed where we want to go. We are willing to accept their help and give our help to others. It is harder to do something alone than together.

FACT: When the lead goose gets tired, it rotates back into the formation, and another goose flies to the point position.
LESSON: It is sensible to take turns doing the hard and demanding tasks and sharing leadership. As with geese, people are interdependent on each other's skills, capabilities and unique arrangements of gifts, talents and resources.

FACT: The geese flying in formation honk from behind to encourage those up front to keep up their speed.
LESSON: We need to make sure our honking is encouraging. In groups where there is encouragement, the production is much greater. The power of encouragement (to stand by one's heart or core values and encourage the heart and core of others) is the quality of honking we seek. We need to make sure our honking is encouraging and not discouraging.

FACT: When a goose gets sick, wounded, or shot down, two other geese will drop out of formation with that goose and follow it down to lend help and protection. They stay with the fallen goose until it dies or is able to fly again. Then, they launch out on their own, or with another formation to catch up with their flock.
LESSON: If we have the sense of a goose, we will stand by our colleagues and each other in difficult times as well as in good!

Developing a Team Vision

A team leader with a vision achieves outcomes and goals that will excite and inspire other members of the team.

To implement a team vision, a leader is able to do the following:

1) **Have a specific vision** – Ask questions. For example: *"What will the final product / outcome look like?"* and *"How will we know when we are successful in completing our task?"*

2) **Develop commitment** – Promote your vision so that team members buy into the vision and commit to it.

3) **Establish trust** – Attempt to reduce all of the fears and risks that are associated with implementing your team vision, as well as working with the selected team members.

4) **Expectations are powerful** – **include everyone** – Expect team members to commit to the team effort and buy into the vision. All team members should feel *ownership* for the team vision.

5) **Encourage collaboration** – Establish a cooperative strategy that emphasizes working together to accomplish the team vision.

How Can You Best Lead?

Effective team leaders . . .

- Work with people and bring out the best in them.
- Transfer ownership of the work to those who will do the work.
- Create an environment in which people want to take responsibility.
- Coach for the development of skills and abilities of team members.
- Encourage team members to collaborate.
- Communicate effectively.

SECTION V:

Team Communicator Scale

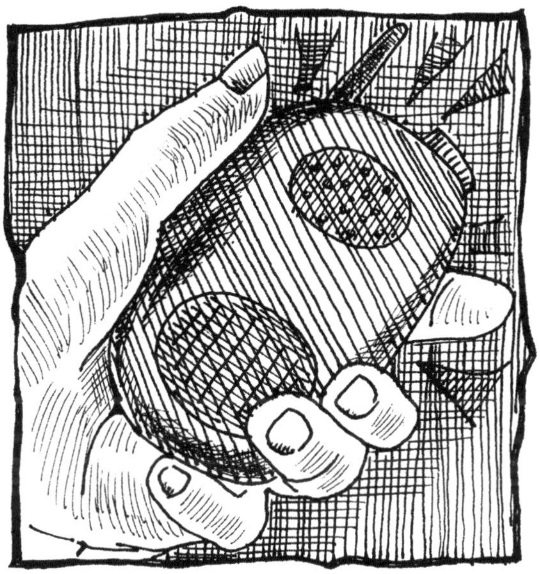

Name____

Date_________________________

Team Communicator Scale Directions

When it comes to team performance, if you do not communicate well, you and the team are at a disadvantage. When you fail to express your ideas clearly and effectively, your ideas usually are not noticed. Communication skills are at the heart of the team process.

The Team Communicator Scale can help you identify how effectively you are able to communicate with other members of your team. This assessment contains 40 statements. Read each of the statements and decide how much you agree with the statement. In each of the choices listed, circle the number of your response on the line to the right of each statement.

In the following example, the circled "Like Me" indicates that the statement describes the person taking the assessment:

SECTION 1: SENDING FEEDBACK

When I am speaking to other team members...

I speak using first person ("I" and "My")	(Like Me)	Not Like Me

This is not a test. Since there are no right or wrong answers, do not spend too much time thinking about your answers. Your initial response will likely be the most true for you. Be sure to respond to every statement.

(Turn to the next page and begin)

Team Communicator Scale

SECTION 1: SENDING FEEDBACK

When I am *speaking* to other team members . . .

I speak using first person ("I" and "My")	Like Me	Not Like Me
I use complete and specific messages	Like Me	Not Like Me
I do not make assumptions	Like Me	Not Like Me
I make sure that my verbal and nonverbal messages are consistent	Like Me	Not Like Me
I repeat my messages in more than one way to ensure understanding	Like Me	Not Like Me
I seek feedback from team members about my message	Like Me	Not Like Me
I match the message to each listener's frame of reference	Like Me	Not Like Me
I describe and name my feelings ("I am frustrated when you . . .)	Like Me	Not Like Me
I describe, but do not evaluate, the behaviors of others	Like Me	Not Like Me
I phrase my messages without talking down to team members	Like Me	Not Like Me

SECTION 2: RECEIVING FEEDBACK

When I am *listening* to other team members . . .

I seek clarification if I do not understand something	Like Me	Not Like Me
I keep my mind open and listen to their suggestions	Like Me	Not Like Me
I try to understand the meaning of each sender's message	Like Me	Not Like Me
I do not interrupt to maximize my understanding of the message	Like Me	Not Like Me
I try not to judge the sender's message or feelings	Like Me	Not Like Me
I relate the message back to the sender in my own words	Like Me	Not Like Me
I try to put myself in the sender's "shoes" to understand the message	Like Me	Not Like Me
I focus totally on what is being said by the sender	Like Me	Not Like Me
I check my perceptions of the sender's feelings by describing them	Like Me	Not Like Me
I try not to communicate my approval or disapproval of the sender's message	Like Me	Not Like Me

(Continued on the next page)

(Team Communicator Scale, continued)

SECTION 3: PROVIDING PERSONAL FEEDBACK

When I am *providing feedback* to other team members . . .

I tell the person how his or her behavior influenced the team	Like Me	Not Like Me
I encourage the person to continue	Like Me	Not Like Me
I encourage the team member to do more	Like Me	Not Like Me
I mention specific behavior or events that were valuable	Like Me	Not Like Me
I tell how his or her behavior made me feel	Like Me	Not Like Me
I give sincere praise	Like Me	Not Like Me
I give public credit when it is due	Like Me	Not Like Me
I give written credit when it is due	Like Me	Not Like Me
I let the person know when I like or approve of something he or she did	Like Me	Not Like Me
I encourage the person by stating how others reacted	Like Me	Not Like Me

SECTION 4: PROVIDING CONSTRUCTIVE CRITICISM

When I am *providing constructive criticism* to other team members . . .

I provide information that can improve his or her behavior	Like Me	Not Like Me
I am perceptive to the person's ability to accept criticism	Like Me	Not Like Me
I word my criticism in ways that are not hurtful	Like Me	Not Like Me
I state specific behaviors that could be improved	Like Me	Not Like Me
I address behaviors, not personality traits	Like Me	Not Like Me
I tell how I feel without being judgmental	Like Me	Not Like Me
I give criticism promptly after an incident	Like Me	Not Like Me
I make my criticism brief and to the point	Like Me	Not Like Me
I try not to cause the other person to feel defensive	Like Me	Not Like Me
I make suggestions, but do not dictate	Like Me	Not Like Me

(Go to the Scoring Directions on the next page)

Team Leader Scoring Directions

The Team Communicator Scale is designed to measure how you send feedback, how you receive feedback, how you provide personal feedback and how you provide constructive criticism. These communication skills are prominent in the team process and make up the four scales for the scale.

To score this scale:

1. Add the number of "Like Me" responses you circled in each of the four sections.

2. Then, transfer your totals for each of the four sections to the corresponding lines below:

SECTION 1: SENDING FEEDBACK TOTAL = ______

SECTION 2: RECEIVING FEEDBACK TOTAL = ______

SECTION 3: PROVIDING PERSONAL FEEDBACK TOTAL = ______

SECTION 4: PROVIDING CONSTRUCTIVE CRITICISM TOTAL = ______

Team Communicator Scale
Profile Interpretation

Total Scale Scores	Result	Indications
Scores from 7 to 10	high	You have the communication skills to be an effective team member.
Scores from 4 to 6	moderate	You have some of the communication skills to be an effective team member.
Scores from 0 to 3	low	You need to develop communication skills to be an effective team member.

For scales which you scored in the **Moderate** or **High** range, find the descriptions on the pages that follow. Then, read the description and complete the exercises that are included. No matter how you scored, low, moderate, or high, you will benefit from these exercises.

(Go to the Scale Descriptions on the next page)

Team Communicator Scale Descriptions

Section 1: SENDING FEEDBACK

People scoring High in this section tend to be proficient at encouraging people on the team to contribute or expand their behaviors. They help team members realize the way their behavior has had a positive influence on other members of the team.

Section 2: RECEIVING FEEDBACK

People scoring High in this section tend to hear what is being offered non-defensively and they consider feedback as an opportunity to learn and self-improve.

Section 3: PROVIDING PERSONAL FEEDBACK

People scoring High in this section tend to be adept at providing feedback to individual members of the team. They are able to give sincere praise and give proper credit to others.

Section 4: PROVIDING CONSTRUCTIVE CRITICISM

People scoring High in this section are able to help other team members receive information about improving or changing his or her behavior. They are able to intuitively know when the recipient is receptive to this feedback, and they are very capable of giving the feedback.

Regardless of your scores on the assessment, you can enhance your team communication by completing the exercises that follow.

Exercises for Enhancing Team Communication

For the exercises in each of the following avtivity handouts, you may provide answers based on a current team of which you are a part, or you may provide answers about a team of which you will be a member in the future.

Show Empathy

Empathy occurs when a team member is able to take the perspective of others and to psychologically step into their shoes and view action from their perspective. Empathy is evident when a team member attempts to understand the feelings, concerns and priorities of other team members.

How will you know when you are showing empathy for other members of the team?

____

____

How important is it to have empathy for members of your team? Why?

____

____

How can you set aside your biases to attempt to enter other peoples' worlds?

____

____

How is empathy different from sympathy?

____

____

How can understanding the feelings of others be helpful to a team?

____

____

How can you begin to show empathy for other members of the team?

____

____

Show Acceptance

- Acceptance of team members is critical in the development of trust.
- Acceptance means showing genuine positive regard for team members including strengths, weaknesses, experiences, talents and unique contributions.
- Acceptance means neither agreeing with team members nor following them blindly.
- Acceptance involves taking people for who they are, not who we want them to be.
- Acceptance of others suggests that you communicate an acceptance of others' attitudes, beliefs, cultural idiosyncrasies, feelings and behaviors.

TEAM MEMBER	WHAT I ACCEPT ABOUT HIM OR HER

Demonstrate Credibility

Credibility means that team members see each other as capable and competent to complete assigned tasks. Credibility suggests that all team members have some talents to bring the team to its conclusion. In the spaces below, list the talents of the other members of your team.

TEAM MEMBER	HIS OR HER TALENTS
Carolyn	*Carolyn has technology skills that could help the team. She has extensive knowledge of Windows and Linux systems administration, can develop websites, and can use programming tools to create programs.*

Addressing Fears and Risks

Identify team members' potential fears about the task.

____

____

____

Identify team members' potential risks about the task.

____

____

____

Send Messages

If interpersonal communications among team members is going to be accurate and effective, it is important to understand the ways in which team members send messages.

Message Tips:

- Phrase messages in such a way that listeners can understand.
- Avoid acronyms and technical information.
- Use a variety of examples and adjust language to each team member.
- Be a credible message sender. Receivers must view your messages as trustworthy and dependable, and based on each member's knowledge about the content being discussed.
- Ask others for feedback regarding their understanding of, and reaction to, what is being communicated.

(Continued on the next page)

(Sending Messages, continued)

In the following spaces, try sending messages to other members of your team:

TEAM MEMBER	HIS OR HER TALENTS
Sharon	*Sharon, when you miss one of our meetings, you miss a lot of information, and we are unable to proceed without your work for the week. Please make it to the next meeting so that we can finish this part of the task. We'd appreciate this.*

Receive Messages

You must be prepared to hear what is being said to you by the other members of the team. How can you prepare yourself to listen more actively?

____

____

____

Keep your mind open and actually listen to what other team members are saying. Listen for understanding and try not to evaluate what is being said. How can you start listening for understanding rather than evaluation?

____

____

____

Try not to interrupt other team members when they are talking. Attempt to hold your desire to react to what others are saying and always think about what you want to say before saying it. What team members are you most likely to interrupt and why?

____

____

____

Confirm your understanding of the messages with the sender right away. This will allow you to seek clarification about confusing aspects of the message. Write an example of a message to confirm understanding.

____

____

____

Seek information from other team members to clarify whether this viewpoint is shared with other members of the team. Write an example of what you will say to other members to be sure the viewpoint is shared by all.

____

____

____

Give Feedback

Feedback prompts members of the team to continue doing things that seem to be working for the benefit of the team. Include team-strengthening feedback to other team members.

- Mention specific behaviors, actions and events that the other team member can understand clearly.
- Tell what you think of the behavior and how it had a positive impact on the other members of the team. Use feeling words to send your message.
- Give sincere praise to the team member.
- Use "I" statements when possible.

In the following spaces, try providing feedback to other members of your team:

PERSON TO WHOM YOU PROVIDE FEEDBACK	MESSAGE
James	*"James, when you found those statistics about organizational change, we were able to develop some great graphs to prove our point! That was the turning point for the team . . . we really got excited about our findings. I appreciate your extra effort to get the stats . . . thanks!"*

Provide Constructive Criticism

Constructive criticism provides information so that other team members can improve or change their behavior. In providing constructive criticism, remember some of the following points:

- Word your feedback so that it does not hurt or damage the team member.
- Identify specific behaviors and situations that need improvement.
- Tell how you feel, but do not include any judgments about other team members.
- Confirm understanding by listening to the person's reaction.
- Offer suggestions on how performance could be improved.

In the following spaces, provide constructive criticism to members of your team:

PERSON TO WHOM YOU PROVIDE FEEDBACK	MESSAGE
Sherry	*"Sherry, I don't sense your commitment to the team or achieving the team goals. I feel frustrated and I am not certain how to motivate you. How can I help you to buy into our vision for the team?"*

Communication Strengths

What do you think are your greatest strengths when communicating with others?

Communication Weaknesses

What do you think are your greatest weaknesses when communicating with others?

Group Leader's Communications

How does your group leader communicate with other members of the team?

Understanding Emotions in Communication

- All communications contain some emotion or mix of emotions
- Emotions can confuse the message one is sending
- Emotions are vital to happiness because they promote action
- Negative emotions can drain your energy and everyone elses
- Positive emotions promote positive communication

Trust

Trust is essential in team communication. Team members build trust through their communications with one another. Trust can be increased or decreased depending on what team members say and do. In order to enhance trust among team members, here are two activities to help build trust:

- Mine Field – Scatter objects in an indoor or outdoor setting. Ask team members to pair up. Have one team member verbally guide her or his partner, who is blindfolded, through the scattered objects.

  Debrief what team members felt.

- Physical Proximity – Have team members pair up. To illustrate the importance of physical proximity, have each pair of team members face each other at a comfortable distance and talk. Then ask people to move a little closer and talk and feel what it is like. Then ask people to increase their distance from each other and talk and feel how it changes feelings and communication.

  Debrief what team members felt.

Whole Person Associates is the leading publisher of training resources for professionals who empower people to create and maintain healthy lifestyles. Our creative resources will help you work effectively with your clients in the areas of stress management, wellness promotion, mental health and life skills.

Please visit us at our web site: **www.wholeperson.com**. You can check out our entire line of products, place an order, request our print catalog, and sign up for our monthly special notifications.

Whole Person Associates

800-247-6789